Henry Coleman

Nippon: A Story of Japan

Henry Coleman

Nippon: A Story of Japan

ISBN/EAN: 9783337171117

Printed in Europe, USA, Canada, Australia, Japan

Cover: Foto ©Andreas Hilbeck / pixelio.de

More available books at **www.hansebooks.com**

NIPPON:

A STORY OF JAPAN

BY
HENRY COLEMAN MAY

NEW YORK:
MDCCCXCVIII.

Nippon; a Story of Japan

CHAPTER I

It was my first morning in Japan. I got up and went to the paper screens and threw them open and in streamed the sunlight—the beautiful sunlight of the Land of the Rising Sun! I had arrived at last! My dream was realized, and I was there.

I had arrived the previous night—in the rain, to my disappointment—and had resolved not to go to the modern European hotel, but to go and stop with a friend who had recently arrived in Japan, and had taken a Japanese house with five Japanese servants and one English valet.

As I gazed out into a most charming little garden, with a miniature pond and most extraordinary dwarfed trees, I heard some one outside my door, and turned around to hear a man-servant (Jokichi I afterward learned was his name) call me to my bath. He spoke broken English, which he thought extremely beautiful, and it was only after some time that I understood what he was saying to me. My bath was a most extraordinary function. I had never taken such a bath in all my life before. The water was about ninety degrees of heat, and I can tell you that it was extremely uncomfortable. After I had finished my bath, all the servants, one by one, took that same boiling tub. When I got back to my room I found my friend waiting to see me. He was dressed and told me that as soon as I was dressed we would go out together; as that day was the festival of armors and flags for boys, being the 5th of

May. I dressed in all haste, and it was not long before I was ready to go out. Outside our house were two kurumas, or jinrickishas, as they are more commonly called. I saw that our (or my friend's) house was a little outside of the city of Tokyo, around which there were very few houses. The place itself was extremely pretty.

We got in our kurumas, and soon our little house was lost to view, and we emerged into the city—a city of doll houses. The first thing I noticed was the enormous fishes set up on a long bamboo pole in front of almost every house. I found out from my guide-book, always my friend, that the fish is a symbol of success for boys. The fish, which is a carp, is called "Shusseuwo," which means fish of success in life. In the shops I saw displayed little figures of warriors in full armor, which were very quaint. I bought a set of them to send to a little fellow who lives across the pond, in America.

We drove through the streets for about an hour and a half. Our jinrickisha men seemed never to get tired. Then we went to the place called Mukojima. It is one of the most beautiful places in Tokyo. It is an avenue of cherry-trees, at this time of the year in full blossom. The avenue is upon the eastern bank of the river Sumida, and is simply magnificent, being a continuous archway of flowers for nearly two miles.

But turn to the southwest and see! There stands the snow-clad Fuji-san, lifting its majestic head high into the azure vault of heaven, as if sanctified for the abode of angels. Fuji-yama, the "matchless mount" indeed! Then look toward the northeast. There yonder you see the majestic Tsukuba, clad in a mantle of purple mist. Above you is a canopy of cherry-blossoms; below you see the river reflecting the expanse of heaven. All along the bank there are scattered kake-jaya, small temporary tea houses. I went into one, and took some of the green tea of Japan. Ugh! what a drink it is! Far from good. I also eat a "sakura-mochi," which are little cakes of rice and pease, wrapped with cherry leaves preserved in salt. They are about as delicious as the tea. After having swallowed these atrocities, we tried to turn our minds from them by hiring a little pleasure boat and gliding up the river. After having passed some time in the boat, we again got in our rickshas and went to take lunch at the Imperial Hotel, where the cuisine is excellent, and European, of course.

CHAPTER II

IN the midst of a nest of old trees in Takanawa, a suburb of Yedo, is hidden Sengakiji, or the Spring Hill Temple, renowned throughout the length and breadth of the land for its cemetery, which contains the graves of the forty-seven Ronins, famous in Japanese history, and heroes in Japanese drama.

On the left-hand side of the main court of the temple is a chapel, in which, surmounted by a gilt image of Kwannon, the goddess of mercy, are enshrined the images of forty-seven men, and of the master whom they loved so well. The statues are carved in wood, the faces painted, and their clothes richly lacquered. Some are old men, with gray and white hair, others are mere boys of sixteen.

Close by the chapel, at the side of a path leading up a hill, is a little well of pure water, fenced in and adorned with a tiny fernery, over which you see an inscription which says: "This is the well in which the head was washed, you must not wash your hands or feet here."

A little further on is a stall at which a man earns his daily bread by selling medals, pictures, and little books, commemorating the loyalty of the forty-seven Ronins. Then higher up yet, shaded by a grove of majestic trees, are forty-eight little tombstones, each decked with evergreens. But there were forty-seven Ronins, and there are forty-eight tombstones?

Yes; and the story of the forty-eighth is truly characteristic of Japanese ideas of honor.

Almost touching the rail of the graveyard is a more imposing monument, under which lies buried the Lord, whose death his followers so piously avenged.

But now the story!

At the beginning of the eighteenth century there lived a Daimio called Asano Takuminokami Naganori, who was lord of the castle of Ako, in the province of Harima. Now it happened that an envoy of the Mikado had been sent to the court of Tokugawa, the Shogun, at Yedo (now called Tokyo). On the arrival of the envoy, Asano and another lord named Kamei Notonokami were appointed to be his entertainers; and a high officer called Kira Kotsukenosuke Yoshihide was ordered to instruct them in the correct ceremonies to be observed on the occasion. Kira was well informed in the ceremonies of the court, and was therefore in great favor, and rose far above the other lords in power.

Now this Kira was a wicked and miserly man at heart, and treated both lords with great disrespect. Kamei at last resolved to kill this impolite lord; and, going home in great anger, told his counselor his idea. At this the counselor was sorely troubled; and, having thought a long time, he resolved to send Kira a gift of money, without telling Kamei anything about it. He put this plan into execution, and sent Kira the money that evening. Kira was delighted, and when the next morning came his manner was greatly changed, and was even so polite that Kamei thought no more of his plan of killing him.

But to Asano, who had sent no money, he was even more impolite, and received him with jeers. At last his manner became so impertinent that Asano as a "Samurai" could no longer stand it, and drawing his dirk he cried to Kira to defend himself; then, aiming at Kira, he cut at him, but only gave him a slight wound on his forehead. By this time the retainers and servants of Kira Kotsukenosuke, hearing the noise of swords and their lord's cries, came running to him, and quickly caught and disarmed Asano. Then all confusion followed, and the news that my lord Asano had attacked his lordship Kira Kotsukenosuke ran like wildfire. Asano was taken into custody, and, after a long trial, it was decided that he should commit seppku (or hara-kiri) for having tried to kill my lord Kira in the precincts of the castle. After Asano was dead his followers became Ronins; that is, "Wandering Samurai without a master"; and forty-seven of them, headed by a man called Oishi Kuranosuke, made a vow that they would kill Kira to avenge the death of their beloved master. They set a day, accordingly, on which they were to meet and march to the yashiki (castle) of Lord Kira, and there to dispatch him without more ado.

Then they dispersed, some becoming workmen, others schoolmasters, and still others learning trades. As for Oishi Kuranosuke, he was leading the life of a drunkard, so as to put Kira off his guard. Once at night, when he was coming home drunk, he fell asleep in the street, and a Satsuma man, coming up, saw him, and spitting on his face and insulting him, said:

"Vile wretch, more beast than Samurai, go! Avenge your lord rather than lie here in the gutter." With these words he went away.

At last Kira was entirely put off his guard, and was rejoicing at the faithlessness (as he thought) of Asano's followers, when the eventful day was drawing near. The day was in December, and the hour which they had fixed upon in which to attack the castle was midnight.

It was the day before the attack, and all the forty-seven had come together to have a farewell feast. At last midnight came, and Oishi Kuranosuke and his men set out for the castle. The weather was freezing and the snow was lying thick upon the ground, but still they marched courageously on.

They have arrived! And now Oishi stands before the yashiki of my lord Kira. His followers, dividing themselves into three parties, attack the gates. The guards are terrified, and run away crying for mercy. The gates give in, and all the forty-seven pour into the yashiki. Kira's men defend themselves bravely, but the Ronins are too much for them, and at last they are conquered. Now Oishi and his men go in search of Kira, who has hid himself. They search and search, and are on the point of despair, when a cry, yes, a call—one of the Ronins has found Kira Kotsukenosuke in a little outhouse! They find him almost dead with fear, and shivering with cold. Then Oishi Kuranosuke goes down on his knees and addresses Kira as follows:

"My lord, we are the retainers of Asano Takuminokami. Last year your lordship and our master quarreled in the palace, and our master was sentenced to hara-kiri, and his family was ruined. We have come to-night to avenge him, as is the duty of faithful and loyal men. I pray your lordship to acknowledge the justice of our purpose. And now, my lord, we beseech you to perform hara-kiri. I myself shall have the honor to act as your second, and when, with all humility, I shall have received your lordship's head, it is my intention to lay it as an offering upon the grave of Asano Takuminokami."

But Kira does not answer a word, but crouches down trembling and wailing. At last Kuranosuke, seeing that it is of no use to urge him, takes his own dirk and cuts off Kira's head.

Then placing it in a bucket, they proceed to Asano's tomb, where they leave it with solemn ceremony, and then report what they have done to the city authorities.

They were ordered, as they expected, to commit hara-kiri, which they performed at the appointed places. Then they were buried honorably by the priests of the temple.

Some time after all this, a Satsuma man came, and, after making prostrations before Asano's and Kuranosuke's tomb, he committed seppku. The priests found him there, and having pity on him, buried him beside the forty-seven Ronins. Thus the forty-eighth.

My friend and I were allowed to inspect the relics, which are in a large room back of the temple. This room opens on one of those wonderful Japanese miniature gardens with dwarfed trees and small rockery in the most fantastic shapes.

The relics are very interesting: old armor made by the Ronins themselves; ragged trousers and sashes, which were once rich silks and brocades; old gold crests and swords; documents written perhaps by Kira himself; old chains;

spears with dark rust marks and dark something else marks; also dirks and broad-swords — innumerable old things that would take a book itself to write them all down in.

At last, tired and weary, we went in our jinrickishas again, flew past everything, till, at last, we stopped in front of our own little door.

CHAPTER III

"GOOD news!" said my friend, as he came into my room. I sat up in my bed and rubbed my eyes. I was still sleepy, and did not like especially to have some one rush into my room and wake me out of a refreshing, dreamless sleep.

"Well," said I, "what news have you got? I'm glad it's good."

"Yes, I've just got a letter from

America, saying that my old friend, Jack Gervaise, is coming over here to the land of Jappy. He will probably be here to-morrow or the day after, as he wrote this letter only a few days before his departure from San Francisco. Won't it be jolly. He's coming here to stop with us—with me. Don't you know him?"

"No," said I, "I have not the pleasure. And the other note, what does it say?" For I saw that he had two notes in his hand.

"Oh! The other is an invitation to lunch to-day with a certain Mr. ——, a Japanese gentleman; rather short notice, but we'll accept, of course, won't we?"

"Of course," said I, eager to go to a Japanese dinner—a real one. "It's going to be 'à la Japonaise,' I suppose?"

"I suppose so; but the card isn't very 'Japonaise,' is it? Going to take a hot bath again this morning?"

"No, thank you. I had rather take it in my own room."

. . . .

We were on our way to dinner. The evening was beautiful; the moon was shining, and the city of Tokyo looked like some fairy scene, red lanterns bobbing up and down like rubies in the dark; children's merry voices ringing out with merry laughter through the clear still night. Everything seemed to say "Peace." It was indeed a charming scene.

At last we arrived at our destination. Our jinrickishas stopped in front of a little avenue leading up to the house, which was not our host's own, but a swell restaurant in which they manage private dinners.

A little "musmée" was at the door,

and bade us enter. After having taken our shoes off, we must have looked lovely in dress-suits and stockinged feet. Our host was a rather elderly gentleman, dressed in the regular costume of the Japanese gentry. We did not go into dinner immediately, as evidently there was somebody else to come. Our expectations were verified. In a few moments an English lady and her daughter came in. Then after them came two Japanese ladies and one Japanese gentleman, the latter dressed in European costume, the former two in the court costume: large full red trousers, trailing behind, white kimonos, and hair arranged heart-shaped on top and flowing loose behind, with a profusion of flowers, in front made of silver paper, and various little ornaments behind. The hair was tied in the middle with gold paper. Both were most picturesque. They spoke English but little, only knowing a few words; but our host spoke it perfectly, as he had been in America a number of years. After a few minutes we all went into the dining-room; the screens opened, and there was our table—flat velvet cushions for each of us. The English lady paled distinctly; so did her daughter. We all seated ourselves as best we could, while the Japanese ladies sank down gracefully, with their faces wreathed in smiles at our attempts.

Then the little musmée entered, and bowing before each, presented us with small handleless cups of most beautiful china. There were little packages beside everybody, which contained chopsticks. I will not attempt to describe the dinner.

This is what we had to eat: Pheasants with feathers stuck all over them, seaweed soup, sakê, and plenty other unnamable things. But in the middle of the dinner there came a pause. One of the sides of the room was pushed open, and in a beautiful little inclosure stood five "Geishas." Three with samisens and two dancing, or rather posturing, forming a series of tableaux. The costumes of the Geishas were gorgeous in the extreme: one was dressed in pink, and the other in a delicate cream color, while the ones who played the samisens were dressed in bright red embroidered with gold. Their hair was profusely bedecked with gold, little sticks, and wonderful imitation flowers. They sang in a nasal falsetto voice, which Europeans cannot appreciate. Their voice is so very unnatural that it must be very painful for them, yet they did not seem to mind it in the least, and finished as fresh as when they began. They hold fans in both hands, and wave them about in a most graceful manner. Then the panels closed up, and we resumed our dinner.

The young English lady, Miss Mabel Elliot, looked perfectly delighted, and she seemed rather sorry when the little performance of the Geishas was over.

Her mother, Mrs. Elliot, who was rather stout, was bordering on insanity, as she had been sitting down à la Japonaise for at least an hour and a half, and it was only after great difficulty that she succeeded in getting up when the dinner was finished.

Our host accompanied us to the door, giving us a most inappropriate handshake. We saw the little Geishas in much more sober clothes out in the garden. When we walked down to our jinrickishas, they looked at us and the two English ladies very curiously, and made some Japanesey remarks about us, as we went away in our kurumas.

The next day I again met Mrs. and Miss Elliot, as my friend and I were visiting the Shiba Daijingu, Temple of Amaterasu-Omikami and Tokoyohime-no-mikoto. I had a chance to talk to Miss, while I let my friend devote himself to the honorable Mrs. She informed me that they were going for a jinrickisha party on the next day, as they had all got their private jinrickishas, and were sure to have good coolies to pull them. She asked me to come. I told my friend, and we decided that we would go.

"Meet to-morrow at 11:30. Don't forget. At the Fugi Jinsha."*

---

* Temple of Konokana Sakuya Hime, the Goddess of the Peak Fujiyama.

CHAPTER IV

FIRST of June! And to-day is our jinrickisha trip. The first thing in the morning that I ask my friend is if our jinrickishas are ordered.

"Kohana!" he cries to the little maid, and claps his hands. In she comes.

"Are our jinrickishas here?"

"Hai!" she says, and bobs out again.

"Very well. Then come on."

Once in our jinrickishas, then ends our conversation, as the law compels kurumas to go behind each other, and not two abreast. It is nothing like 11:30 yet, so I resolve to spend my time in shopping. Shopping is not the word for buying things in Japan. It is too commonplace for all those dainty things set out before you; one would like to buy everything at once.

"Here, stop!" I cry in my best Japanese to my ricksha man, as I see a show before me that I cannot resist. He stops and I go in. My friend follows me. Here I see a beautiful kimono, evidently old and very valuable. I have not got one yet, so I *must* get it. "Ikura?" ("How much?"), I ask the man, pointing to it.

"Hyaku-yen-de-gozarimas" ("It is a hundred yen"), says he, smiling and bowing at me.

"Is it dear or not?" I ask my friend. "I know nothing in the prices of kimonos."

"Neither do I," is the unsatisfactory answer.

"Well, I'll take it; and here is the money," I say to the man, who seems delighted. He wraps it up for me, and I send it out to my jinrickisha.

I have only got three yen left now. I just brought with me one hundred and three yen. I want to spend it. I look around some time; and at last see an obi—just what I want to go with the kimono.

"Ikura?"

Three and a half yen, and I've only got three left. I borrow a half from my friend and buy it, and send it off also to my jinrickisha.

My friend has bought more than I

have. He has a sword, Japanese pipe, one Buddha, and one very modern kimono, and a beautiful sword hilt.

We stayed some time in this little shop, and the merchant displayed some of his most precious things, stowed away and wrapped up in brown and yellow cloth. One of his most beautiful things was an ancient kimono of yellow and gold.

This "velly oll," he told us, as he showed it to us. We gazed at it admiringly, and then abruptly took our leave, as the temptation to "*buy*" was becoming very alarming. Then we rolled through the streets on our way to our meeting-place, the temple of Fuji Jinja. The first day of June is the festival of the goddess of Fujiyama, and therefore we chose her temple as our rendezvous. Men sell straw serpents to the multitude on that day, as is the old custom. This temple once belonged to the Daimyo of Kaga.

When we arrived we went immediately to the very spot appointed for our meeting; but, to our surprise, neither Mrs. nor Miss Elliot were to be seen, and it was already after the time appointed. We waited for about a half an hour, when we concluded that mademoiselle had calmly changed her mind, and had not the faintest notion of coming; but we were mistaken, for just when we were preparing to go back home in came both Miss and Mrs., and others besides, in a most preposterous hurry. When she got near us she explained that the jinrickisha man she had engaged fell ill, and she had the hardest time in getting another who would go for such a long way; but after great difficulty she had succeeded in getting this man, who seemed perfectly good.

We got out of our rickshas and walked around the temple grounds, and also went in the temple. It was very crowded; but as the day was rather cool it was not uncomfortable. All the young girls had donned their holiday attire, and very pretty they looked, with their bright obis (sashes) and varicolored kimonos. The elder women wore rather more sober colors, such as gray and dark purple, and the men were dressed entirely in dark blues, blacks and grays; though I occasionally saw one or two in green or mauve. Altogether it was a most interesting scene. After staying some time we thought it about time to set out, so we all came back to our jinrickishas, and off we went.

The streets were almost deserted, as every one had gone to the temple that day. The drive to get into the country is not long, and we were soon out of the city. The scenery was beautiful, and Miss Elliot had her sketch-book with her. Every now and then, when we wanted to jot down some pretty little house with a thatched roof or a rice field with peasants about, we would stop and sketch the object of our fancy.

We did not travel very quickly, as we saw many pretty little bits.

When we got further out in the country the peasants would stare at us. They do not often see foreigners where we went, as we did not take the regular road. At last we thought that we would stop to take lunch, and all halted by a little brook. There were two little children who were sitting down by a tree not very far away. They watched us eat with great curiosity. We did not have much of a lunch—boiled eggs, rice biscuits, sandwiches, apollinaris and beer. We were a jolly party altogether, and had lots of fun. There was an especially funny old English gentleman, some relation of the Elliots, I believe; also a rather stiff young lady, highly uninteresting; and her brother, about twenty-two years, also of rare stupidity.

Miss E—— tried to coax the small children who were watching us to come to us, but in vain; at last she got up and began to run after them to their terror. They shrieked and ran wildly away, their small kimonos floating in the air behind them. They ran toward a little clump of bushes on the border of a wood, out of which suddenly came a woman with a small baby on her back. She seemed very angry that we should torment her darlings. We explained, through one of our jinrickisha men, who spoke fairly good English, that we simply wanted to see the children nearer, as we thought them very sweet and charming. This pacified the woman immediately, and she even became quite friendly; she even brought the two children, now calm, to come and see us. They looked at us in wonderment and reverence, as if we were some extraordinary creatures descended from some Buddhist heaven. We now became quite interested in the woman, and inquired where she lived. We found that she had a little house not far away. We went as far to ask her if we could visit her house. She answered "Hai" immediately, and seemed highly enchanted that she should have the honor of our visiting her home. We had finished lunch by this time, and resolved that we would walk to the house, while our ricksha men smoked their tiny little pipes.

Then off we started, the woman

leading the way, while jolly old Mr. Fenwick asked her many questions through his guide-book; but she only stared, for I do not think his accent was of the best Japanese or his grammar quite correct. He was not to be discouraged though, and took to something easier, and after making a wild excursion through his note-book, he politely asked her, "If there was any place to be seen about this town?" Which in Japanese is "Kono-hen ni nanika kembutsu suru monowa arimasen ka."

This time she laughed, and must

have thought that foreigners had very queer minds, as there was no town for at least seven miles, as we were just about that from Tokio. Still she did not answer him, and he gave up in despair.

Soon the house hove in view. It was quite large, and had a thatched roof. The house, as all Japanese houses, was not built on the ground, but on posts which rest on large flat stones, so that if any severe wind comes the house will not fall down, but will rock upon these large stones. It is also a precaution against earthquakes, which are very frequent in Japan. We all took off our shoes, as is customary before entering houses in Japan, for the big clogs of the Japanese would spoil the delicate soft greenish-white matting, which is the covering for each floor.

The house was very neat, and flowers were seen here and there, tastefully arranged in vases. The woman was fairly well off, we could see, and had some very pretty little things. There was a little Daikoku sitting on a red lacquered stool, which was particularly captivating; there were flowers arranged about him—about little fat person, smiling good-naturedly. Daikoku is the god of wealth, and almost all Japanese families keep a little statue or picture of him, and reverence him a great deal. There was a panel with Fuji-yama painted on it, which was also very pretty.

Our hospitable hostess made us understand that she was going to give us some tea. It was quite a long time before we understood what she meant; but at last she kept on repeating "cha" and "cha" again. Mr. Fenwick hunted in his guide-book and radiantly told us that it was "tea!" Then he said "Hai," and before we could say anything, she was off to get green tea, without either cream or sugar. She soon appeared again bearing seven cups on a little tray of black lacquer, or at least imitation lacquer. The wicked Mr. Fenwick chuckled at the mischief he had done, as he knew none of us would have the heart to refuse the tea that our smiling hostess had brought. *She* thought that it was a treat she was giving us, and would be surprised and pained if we should refuse it, of course.

But we all drank it down in a gulp, as if it was the sweetest drink imaginable, though she must have thought Europeans were very gluttonous, to swallow it down in such manner, instead of daintily sipping it as her countrywomen do. After the *tea* she entertained the ladies by exhibiting her kimonos and quilts; her finest, of course.

We learned that she kept boarders overnight — those that passed on the road, traveling to some other place; but she had nobody at present, and her house was quite empty.

Then came an idea! We could pass the night there, and resume our jinrickisha voyage in the morning! The house was empty, and consequently there was lots of room. But how tell her?

We decided that some one should go and bring Toko, the ricksha man, who could speak English, to come and propose this to the mistress of the house. Accordingly I set out to get him, and in a short time returned, Toko pulling me in his jinrickisha.

He told her our intention, which she received with exclamations of happi-

ness, that we, the "honorable foreigners," "would deign to stop overnight in her humble home." Provision was also made for our coolies, who were to sleep in a little outhouse, rather old and broken down, but still good enough.

Our entertaining hostess now announced that her two little girls were going to give us a little amusement. We were certainly having a delightful evening, one of my most delightful evenings in Japan. From the open blinds we could see the sun setting; the sky was a beautiful golden red, specked with little bluish clouds, and two little birds were flying around and twittering in the sky. Then noiselessly the sun sank down to rest, and the golden red faded into pink, then pale yellow, and then the sky became again a mantle of darkish blue, and the two little birds went to their nest. None of us spoke, so beautiful was this scene, till our hostess's merry voice broke the silence, announcing that the performance was to begin. She brought with her two wood and paper lamps, which she set down on the floor about ten feet apart. After her came in two little bodies, which, through their paint, we recognized as the two little girls of the afternoon. They looked different indeed. Instead of the simple little gray and brown kimonos which we first saw them in, they were gaudily attired in light blue with lozenge patterns—flowers and birds all over their little kimonos. They wore sashes of bright red, and their faces were painted and powdered like veritable little coquettes, yet they were rather shy, which did not go at all with their appearance. They began a song, which lasted about fifteen minutes. It was not at all the voices which you hear from Geishas and professional singers, and it was much more pleasing to the ear, as it was neither strained nor nasal. Their voices, indeed, were very sweet and soft and low; they did not get excited and begin to make gestures, and jump around, but kept motionless, standing with their little hands hidden in their sleeves.

When the song was over, they gave a sort of little pantomime, clapping their hands and stamping their feet, and twirling around. The two funny little bodies began twisting themselves around in most extraordinary shapes, and afforded us a considerable amount of amusement. But the young, uninteresting lady seemed perfectly serious, and was jotting down things in her note-book; her brother, however, lost a little of his dignity, to our great surprise. He actually even made quite a bright remark, to our still greater surprise. Suddenly our two little entertainers dropped to their knees, and touched their flower - bedecked little heads to the ground, and, getting up, quietly glided out of the room. We clapped them vigorously, and their proud mother followed them out of the room, only to appear again to show us our rooms, which were four in all. I had one with my friend, Miss Elliot with her mother, and Mr. Fenwick with the uninteresting young gentleman, and the uninteresting lady had a room to herself. She requested, from her guide-book, to the landlady, that she wished four under-quilts to sleep on, while we contented ourselves (excepting Mrs. Elliot) with two, though we all lived to regret it, as the next morning we had the most violent pains in our shoulders. The night was very warm, so I slept with my paper blinds open.

It was a beautiful night. I could see the moon shining down upon the rather large garden outside of my window, or rather of my paper blinds thrown open. Everything looked so enchanting outside that I really could *not* get to sleep. I hated to close my eyes on this lovely and quiet scene, and I at last succumbed to the temptation to go out in the garden, so putting on a rather worn kimono which I found in the room, I quietly slipped out, and took a little fifteen-minute walk around about the house. Then, returning, I again got into my quilts, and slept the sleep of the just.

. . . . . .

I awoke early in the morning to hear the laughter of the little children of the house, who were amusing themselves with their younger brother, out in the garden, immediately outside my window. They were at a well with a little wooden bucket in their hands. They were sending it down and bringing it up again full of water. Then they would dump the water in again and begin the same over again. They

kept this up for some time, and when they had finished I saw them turn toward me. They saw my blinds were open, and advanced nearer. I made believe to be asleep. Then the little inquisitive bodies were assured, as they thought I really was. The eldest spoke in a whisper to the two others; then, leaving them at some distance, she clambered up the little piazza which surrounded the house, and came toward my window. First she gave a long look in, and then, thinking I was asleep, she advanced in my room. I was in perpetual fear that my friend would awake and thereby frighten the little visitor away. He did not awake, but he suddenly turned around, which set Miss Inquisitive flying off, leaping off piazza and all, and falling in a heap on the grass. The other little girl ran to her help, but the baby brother sat down, or rather tumbled down, on the grass, and smilingly observed the proceedings.

It was time that I should dress, so I got up and closed the shutters. My friend was also awake by this time, and after having performed our ablutions, we were in a short time out of our room.

In less than twenty-five minutes everybody was out and ready to depart. We did not eat much breakfast, except rice and peaches, which our hostess provided. We bid her "sayonara," and paying her her money, to which we added a few yen, we rolled off in our kurumas, to resume our journey.

CHAPTER V

THE next afternoon, when we arrived home, a pleasant surprise was awaiting us. As soon as we entered our little house we found that my friend's dear friend, Jack Gervaise, was inside waiting for us. We hurried into the next room, where we fond him reading a novel. After having exchanged salutations with my friend, he was introduced to me. He was a charming fellow, and was also very handsome. He had a small blonde mustache and very light blonde hair. We spent the whole evening in interesting conversation. The next night we all went to see the Japanese theater, to see Danjuro, Japan's greatest actor. We were all settled in the theater when the play began. In came the actors, down the polished, flowery way — a sort of long platform which serves as an exit and entrance for them. The costumes of the actors were something magnificent. Danjuro, in this play, took the part of a woman, as women are not allowed to play in Japan on the stage, except one actress, a Madam Yone Nachi, who plays in a theater with women only. Danjuro's make-up was simply wonderful. It was impossible for one to tell him from a woman; his face was painted white and then rouged; his eyebrows were exquisitely arched, and his mouth was exceedingly small, and was vermillion red, with a dash of gold across his chin. The scene of the play was laid in the Yoshiwara, and, of course, we did not understand a word of it.

At last the play ended, and the actors again paraded out on the "Flowery Way." We all had enjoyed it very much, and were really sorry when it was over. The audience had been also an amusement, whole families dressed in their best, looking on with every emotion portrayed in their faces; and in between the acts almost everybody was seen smoking their tiny pipes, which only hold about three puffs, and which also they are constantly refilling.

We had a most delightful walk home —my friend, Mr. Gervaise and I. It was a moonlight night, clear and still —one of those beautiful June nights when one would like to stay out all night. But, alas! we soon arrived home, and in a few minutes were too sleepy to be sentimentally inclined.

Two days after I left Tokyo to visit Nagoya, Yokohama and Nagasaki, which were all very delightful. Nagoya was extremely interesting on account of the old palace-castle which is there. This old structure is something wonderful, and I spent hours in it.

Some of the walls have most remarkable frescoes on them, which are very, very old. I have never seen fresco work in Japan, except this, and I believe it *is* the only piece of any consequence in the whole country. Nagasaki was also charming. The scenery around the Inland Sea is beautiful beyond description.

Girls in bright attire, with brilliant kerchiefs on their heads, stroll the streets of Nagasaki with samisens in their hands every night. They sing and tell funny stories or ghost stories, and usually they attract great crowds. The Geishas of Nagasaki are rather famous.

I did not like Yokohama quite so much, though there is no doubt that it is a lovely city, and has many charming spots. But I really was glad to return to old Tokyo, of which I have grown really fond.

A most astounding piece of news awaited my arrival. As soon as I was home again my friend calmly told me that Jack Gervaise was engaged to be married to Miss Mabel Elliot!

"What!" I exclaimed. "Engaged after a month and a half's acquaintance!"

But I found that they had known

each other for years in old England, and *that* must have been Mr. Gervaise's reason for coming to Japan.

They were married in Paris two months after, and I am sorry to say that I was not at the wedding, as by that time I was again in New York.

And now, when I sit by my fireside in the evenings, I often fall asleep and dream of that far-away land—that enchanting land of the rising sun—that land of the chrysanthemum—that land which will always be a sweet memory to me. That land of Japan!

So then, "Sayonara."

www.ingramcontent.com/pod-product-compliance
Lightning Source LLC
Chambersburg PA
CBHW020300090426
42735CB00009B/1151